FIRENZE
MVSEI

Pitti Palace
Modern Art
Gallery

CARLO SISI
Director of the Modern Art Gallery

sillabe

© 1999 Ministero per i Beni e le Attività Culturali -
Soprintendenza per i Beni Artistici e Storici di Firenze, Pistoia e Prato

A pubblication of
s i l l a b e s.r.l.
piazza Damiano Chiesa, 49 - 57124 Livorno
tel. 0586.867034 - fax 0586.869119

managing editor: Maddalena Paola Winspeare
graphic design and cover: Laura Belforte
editing: Bettina Müller
translation: Anthony Cafazzo
translation of the introduction: Harriet Paterson, Marina Pugliano

series design: Franco Bulletti
photolithography: La Nuova Lito-Firenze

reproduction rights:
Archivio sillabe/Foto Remo Bardazzi
Archivio Fotografico SBAS Firenze
Foto Brogiolo, Brescia
Foto Saporetti, Milano

ISBN 88-86392-84-2

SUMMARY

Enough books have been written about the public museums in Florence run by the Fine Arts and Historic Works Commission to fill a large library. This is hardly surprising when one considers that the artistic heritage preserved in our museums has been famous throughout the world for centuries. For hundreds of years writer and scholars, travellers of every nationality and country have been attempting to describe all that the Florentine museums contain. They have made great efforts to explain why these museums are so fascinating, and to lead a path through paintings and sculptures for both the uninformed but willing visitor and the refined and jaded intellectual.

Over time, however, the museums have altered their aspect and their layout, the exhibitions have been arranged in new ways, the collections have been enriched (or impoverished). Attributions of works in the museums have also changed, restorations have transformed the appearance of many pieces, the rise and fall of aesthetic tendencies have led to reorganisation and the exhibition of differing works. All these things are constantly taking place within the public collections because museology and the history of art, like any intellectual endeavour, are in a constant state of progress and transformation. This explains why the literature surrounding the Florentine museums (like that of any of the world's great art collections) is so immense, and in a process of continual updating and change.

The perfect, definitive guide to a museum, any museum, does not and cannot exist.

The premise seems obvious, but is nonetheless necessary in order to understand the point of the publication introduced by these lines. From the moment when, in accordance with the application of the Ronchey law 4/93, the Giunti publishing house group took over the running of the support services within the Florentine museum system, it was decided to start at once on a standardised series of illustrated guides. These guides, displaying the cuneiform flower of "Firenze Musei" on the cover, guarantee that at the year of publication the state of each museum is exactly that described in the guide.

Certain things are obviously necessary if a museum guide is to aspire to reliability, official standing and at the same time enjoy a wide distribution: accuracy of information, high quality reproductions, an easily manageable format, a reasonable cost and – not least – a clearly written text (without, naturally, being banal or lacking in precision). Readers will judge for themselves if the guide which follows this introduction reaches these standards. I have no doubt that this will be a serious and committed judgement, just as myself and the Publisher of this guide have been serious and committed in attempting to meet the cultural needs of whoever visits our museums in the best way and with every possible care.

Antonio Paolucci
*Head of the Fine Arts
and Historic Works Commission
of Florence, Pistoia and Prato*

Modern Art Gallery
The birth a museum

The history of the Gallery begins in about 1748, when the grand duke Pietro Leopoldo of Lorraine began the remodelling of the Florentine Academy, establishing a Modern Art Gallery in its interior (next to the classical art collection made up of works once suppressed by ecclesiastical bans). The gallery was to contain the paintings and sculptures that received awards in academic competitions, as well as entries in the *pensionato artistico* contests. In those same years, due to the need to decorate Pitti Palace, works of art were being collecting by order of the grand duke. By the middle of the 19th century, they were already so numerous that was necessary to transfer many of them to the Crocetta Palace (which today houses the Archaeological Museum), which was thus destined, in these early years, to become the new Modern Art Museum. The project was interrupted due to the expulsion of the Lorraine in 1850, but the uni-

fication government hastened to provide an official home for the major Florentine collections of modern art. A debate was in fact underway at the time regarding the position of the Academy of Fine Arts as a scholastic institution and the possibility of establishing a museum there. In concomitance with the reform of 1867, all the works of the Lorraine collections were thus brought together in the Modern Gallery of the Academy, as the new institute came to be called, while those more linked to pedagogy were destined for the school.

As had already occurred during the Lorraine era, the House of Savoy also became interested in acquiring modern works of art for the apartments of Pitti Palace. This was especially true of Vittorio Emanuele II, who enlarged the collections with paintings, sculptures and decorations that had inspired admiration during the exhibits of the time, beginning with the 1861 World Fair in Florence celebrating the Unification of Italy. To supplement the major collections of the Academy and the Savoys, towards the century's end, a policy of

Luigi Catani, Presentation of the discovery of the telescope in Venice *and*
A classroom of the University of Science, *room 11.*

acquisitions was begun by the Florence City Council, which in 1867 took possession of a collection of *macchiaioli* paintings that had belonged to Diego Martelli. It was then that the idea was advanced of uniting the city's modern art collections. The aim was to historically consolidate the art of the recent past with the important contributions of the *macchiaioli* and works of national contemporary art, whose acquisition had been under the guidance of an active municipal commission between 1901 and 1910. Thus, in 1914 the Italian State and the Florence City Council reached an agreement on the administration of the nascent Modern Art Gallery, in which the various collections would be brought together, irrespective of their ownership (state or municipal). The convention moreover set up a specific Commission of experts to oversee acquisitions. With regards to physical site, the hypothesis emerged of locating the Gallery in Pitti Palace, an idea that was realised in 1922, when the royal family vacated the second-floor apartments.

The first lay-out was inaugurated in 1924 and, as described by Jahn Rusconi in his *Guida* to the museum published in 1934, the artistic itinerary favoured the most recent aspects of art, beginning with the *macchiaioli*, thereby foregoing the figurative documents of neo-classicism and romanticism. From then up to the 1970s, the Gallery would experience a broad expansion, mainly through addition of 20th-century collections. The art housed in the Gallery today is the result of the regular purchases of the Commission in the period between the two world wars, the continuous stream of works destined by statute to the Gallery, as well as those having received the contemporary art awards of the annual Fiorino exhibit. However its resources are far from static. Still today, the incessant flow of loans and donations is testament to the vital presence of the Modern Art Gallery within Florence's museum system.

The visit

The current museum collection comprises thirty rooms that trace a wide chronological arc: from the time of Pietro Leopoldo up to the First World War. The tour, organised in chronological order and by historical-topical category, attempts to furnish the visitor with a clear view of the histories of the various core collections and enable a correct reading of the diverse atmospheres, marked as they are by the personal tastes of the royal families alternating in their reigns. These comprise the second-floor rooms of Pitti Palace which have been passed on to us in their original Lorraine arrangement, attributed mainly to Pasquale Poccianti, except for rooms 14, 15 and 16, in which the roofs decorated in the time of Ferdinando II de' Medici are still conserved. The *suite* on the facade side (rooms 17-25) was called the "District of the Arch-duchesses", while the rooms that give on to the patio up to the Ballroom constituted the "New District" (rooms 1-7), which led to the apartment called the "Bourbon or New Palatine" (rooms 8-13). The roofs of some of these rooms were decorated during the Restoration by some of Tuscany's major artists: Giorgio Berti, *Cincinnatus receiving the Roman Senate* (room 7); Niccola Monti, *The Victory of the True Cross* (room 8); Gaspare Martellini, *Tu Marcellus eris* (room 9); Luigi Catani, *Facts and personages of Philosophy and Science* (rooms 10-11); Giuseppe Bezzuoli, *Alessandro in Apelle's study* (room 12); Antonio Luzzi, *Achilles brought by Tetis to Chiron the Centaur* (room 13).

Niccola Monti, The Victory of the True Cross, *room 8*,
Giuseppe Bezzuoli, Alessandro in Apelle's study, *room 12*.

ROOM 1

Aspects of neo-classicism in Tuscany

With the remodelling of the Fine Arts Academy initiated by Pietro Leopoldo in 1784, Florence was endowed with an institute of artistic instruction modernised according to the standards of international neo-classicism and as renowned as those of Vienna or Milan, likewise of Habsburg origin. It is in this environment, that late Baroque aesthetics are to be transcended in Tuscany, thanks to the teachings, amongst others, of Santi Pacini and Pietro Pedroni; to the presence of Pompeo Batoni; to the 'classicising' tastes of Francesco Carradori and Stefano Ricci; and to the renewed figurative culture underlying the grand duke's acquisition of Gaspare Landi's paintings and some foresighted commissions, such as the famous statue, Abandoned Psyche *that Medici Lenzoni charged to Pietro Tenerani, magisterially ratifying the neo-classical primacy of ideal beauty and a style that was to find success throughout all spheres of art even during the years of the Restoration.*

**POMPEO GIROLAMO
BATONI**
*Hercules at the
crossroads*
Oil on canvas, 93.5 × 73 cm

This painting, together
with its companion
piece, *The child Her-
cules choking a serpent,*
was acquired specifical-
ly for Pitti Palace by

grand duke Ferdinando
III in 1818. Commis-
sioned by the Gerini
family in 1740 and car-
ried out in 1742, it rep-
resents a elegant exam-
ple of the ongoing shift
from the rococo style to
the formal order of neo-
classicism, confirming
Batoni as the Tuscan
founder of the classicist

trends that characterise,
even in Florence, the
figurative culture of the
first decades of the 19th
Century. In fact, it was
by consciousness of this
modernity, that the
grand duke reserved
the works of this Luccan
painter for the Palace
decorations, rather than
for the rooms of the

Royal Gallery, thus acknowledging Batoni's eminent role in the ongoing evolution of art in its passage from 18th-century style and grace to the recovery of classical methodology.

PIETRO TENERANI
Abandoned Psyche
Marble, h. 118 cm

This is the first marble version made from the mould, today in the "Museo di Roma", carried out between 1816 and 1817 and later reproduced with some variation by Tenerani himself on commission for Italian and foreign collectors. The Florentine version belonged to the house of Medici Lenzoni, where it earned the admiration of Niccolini, Leopardi and Lorenzo Bartolini, that is to say, the *élite* of classical romanticism, who probably saw the work as the highest translation of those concepts that, in literature as well as art, were undermining the rigid canons of neo-classicism. Already from the second decade of the century, we begin to see the integration of more flexible observations on nature and its multiple manifestations, along the lines of the incipient aesthetics of Purism.

Primacy of French Art between the Revolution and the Empire

The occupation of Florence by Napoleon's troops in 1807, and the advent of the Grand Duchy of Elisa Baciocchi were political episodes of great moment, affecting the development of the arts in Tuscany, as well. The French court that had settled in Pitti Palace immediately revealed their sensitivity and propensity to promoting taste, assigning commissions in all branches of the arts. The indisputable leaders of this brief but prolific period were Pietro Benvenuti, who Elisa named director of the Academy of Fine Arts, the French painters – Boguet, Gauffier, Fabre and Gagneraux – who emigrated from Rome at the end of the 18th Century, and Antonio Canova, pride of the court, whose contributions to the Palace collection included the bust of Calliope and the Italian Venus, sculpted in order to compensate the Florentines for the loss of the de' Medici collection transferred to France. In order to celebrate this 'Athens of Italy', the selfsame Benvenuti executed the large painting of Elisa amongst the artists, destined for Versailles and thanks to which we can document, not only the presence of these illustrious personages, but also the elegance of the interior decoration which the French had remodelled, introducing to Pitti Palace notable examples of Empire furniture.

PIETRO BENVENUTI

*The oath of the
Saxons to
Napoleon*

Oil on canvas, 380×480 cm

The painting was commissioned by order of the Napoleonic Civil List probably after a journey by Benvenuti to Paris in 1809. It was destined for the Palace of Versailles along with other paintings that Napoleon had charged to major European artists in celebration of his own military feats. In 1812 it was exhibited in the Gallery of the Academy of Fine Arts in Florence before being sent to France. Without a doubt the sensational aspect of the painting is the night-lighting effect that Benvenuti choose to impart dramatic elements to the scene which could temper the encomiastic theme and, at the same time, testify to the artist's command of the pre-romantic aspects of contemporary figurative culture. In 1815 the grand duke Ferdinando III would send Benvenuti to Paris as emissary to reclaim the works of Tuscan art that the French had requisitioned. It was on this occasion that the painting was returned and, after changing hands a number of times, was acquired by the Italian state in 1914.

ANTONIO CANOVA
Calliope
Marble, h. 46 cm

This idealised head was sculpted in 1812, commissioned by Giovanni Rosini who, as testified to by Isabella Teotochi Albrizzi, kept it on display in his house in Pisa in a small temple consecrated to the fine arts, an emblem of classicist idealism to which the man of letters had dedicated his life's work. The sculpture was acquired in 1855 by the director of the Royal Gallery of Florence, who exchanged it with the bust of Rosini that Tenerani had sculpted at the express request of his son, and sent to the Modern Gallery of the Academy, whence it would later be transferred to Pitti Palace. The refined execution of the head, with the pliant tenderness and elegant varieties in the rendering of the hair and ribbon crossing the forehead is proof of Canova's authorship and a valid argument in allowing identification of the work as the "Muse" often referred to in the sculptor's correspondence with Rosini and others.

Louis Gauffier

Self-portrait with his wife and two children

Oil on canvas,
72.5 × 54.5 cm

The artist resolved the theme as a group of whole figures within a landscape of evident classicist suggestion continuing in the style of the valued *conversation pièce* in demand with the bourgeois commissions of those years. The background, with the temple and high marble base on which leans Gauffier's wife, Paolina Chatillon – also his pupil and, according to records at Pitti, author of artist's figure that appears to the right – confirms the painter's adhesion to neo-classical canons. Gauffier, well-known mainly for his compositions of the historical and mythological genre, had lived in Villa Medici and was forced to flee to Florence during the anti-French uprisings.

Room 3

Iconography of pre-unification Tuscan dynasties: the Habsburg-Lorraine, the Bourbons of Lucca, Maria Beatrice d'Este, Duchess of Massa

The paintings, sculptures and objects that have remained in the decorations and the storeroom of Pitti Palace allow us today to journey through the early 19th-century succession of dynasties up to the government of Tuscany. We can thus trace the evolution of trends in taste and the principles of art determined by the various commissions carried out for the Palace, as the rooms were modernised with prestigious European furniture and decorations. The portraits of the sovereigns, from Pietro Leopoldo to Ferdinando III, from Napoleon to the queen of Etruria, from Elisa Baciocchi to Leopoldo II, all recall the various phases of Florentine history between the French Revolution and the Unification of Italy, while the decorations of priceless execution testify to the attention that those taking over the city's government had devoted to progress.

FRANÇOIS-XAVIER FABRE

Portrait of Maria Luisa of Bourbon, queen of Etruria.

Oil on canvas, 58 × 45.5 cm

Regent of the Grand Duchy of Tuscany on behalf of her son from 1803 to 1807, the 'infanta' Maria Luisa of Bourbon is depicted by Fabre with the insignias and jewels for which the queen is said to have nurtured an maniacal passion. The painting demonstrates the artist's observance of neo-classical cannons and was executed as a study for the official portrait of the Bourbon family carried out between 1801 and 1804. A refugee with other French citizens in Florence in 1793 after the Roman rebellions, here the painter became acquainted with the countess d'Albany and eventually court artist for Elisa Baciocchi. Fabre distinguished himself mainly as a portrait artist, though Lord Bristol provided him with the occasion to try his hand at the historical genre, charging him, in 1800, with *Filottete* and the *Judgement of Salomon.*

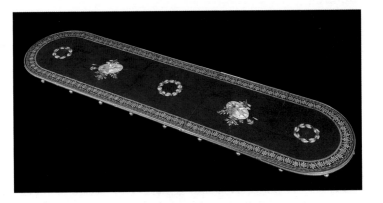

Table centrepiece

1807-16
Lapislazuli with chalcedony mosaics, pearls and gilded bronze ornamentation,
298 × 73 cm

It was Maria Luisa of Bourbon who in 1807 initiated the creation of this magnificent ornament, entrusting its execution to the extraordinary skills of artisans then active at the Grand Duchy's Gallery of Works. The exquisite materials, such as the lapislazuli, were set in an original decoration containing more than a thousand inlaid pearls. At its inception, the work was destined for Napoleon, whose initials were inscribed in a crown of laurel in the central area of the piece, as appears in a first draft of the work by Carlo Carlieri. After being sent to France by Elisa Baciocchi, this so-called *dessert* was returned to Ferdinando III who, in 1816 had the work completed, ordering all signs of Napoleon to be eliminated and adding the chiselled bronze work by Andrea Fondelli.

ROOM 4

The Demidoff in Florence and the art of the Restoration

In the years of the Restoration, the presence of the Demidoff family in Florence had profound influences on the cultural balance of the city. The lifestyle that the Russian princes led in the spectacular residence of San Donato was almost a challenge to the Tuscan aristocrats and the court of the Grand Duchy itself. The mindfulness that they demonstrated to all genres of art was unrivalled, a fact attested to by the extraordinary breadth of their collections. Theirs is also the merit of having fostered in Tuscany awareness of French historical painting – Ingres, Delacroix, Delaroche – and providing impetus to the development of the applied arts, especially the historicist furnishings of Falcini and Frullini. Perhaps their most important contributions are the many works they commissioned to Lorenzo Bartolini and Giuseppe Bezzuoli, who in those years represented the acme of the new poetics of romanticism.

LORENZO BARTOLINI

Model of the monument to Nicola Demidoff

Marble, h. 200 cm

This is the model of the monument that Anatolio and his brother Paolo wished to erect to their Father, Nicola along the Lungarno alle Grazie, near the public institutes sponsored by the family – an act of philanthropy very much appreciated by the moderate Tuscans and the Vieusseux Cabinet. Exhibited in Paris in 1840, it was subsequently sent to the villa of San Donato, and finally to the Villa Pratolino when the property was acquired by the Demidoff in 1872.

The allegory of the monument, alluding to the moral qualities of Nicola and his civic and cultural generosity, is represented by the statues of the pedestal, sculpted with the natural grace that characterises the stage of transition from neo-classical abstraction to the uneasy truths of Purism.

ARY SCHEFFER

*Portrait of the
princess Matilde
Bonaparte Demidoff*

Oil on canvas, 176 × 89.5 cm

From the collection of
the Demidoff princes
that was kept on display
in the villa of San Do-
nato and later in Pra-
tolino, the painting was
donated by Paolo Kara-
georgevich to the Flo-
rentine Galleries in
1969. Princess Matilde
(1820-1904), who was
educated in Rome and
Florence, married Ana-
tolio Demidoff in 1840
and left him in 1846 in
order to go and live in
Paris, where during the
time of Napoleon III she
would kept the most
frequented drawing-
room in the capital.
Scheffer painted this
portrait in 1844, keep-
ing well in mind, in
both its design and
composition, the fa-
mous models of Ingres.
It was framed only later
by the Pacetti brothers
in Florence, who
demonstrated great
skill in engraving the
frame's ornamental
motif in the form of lau-
rels.

GIUSEPPE BEZZUOLI
Christ borne to the Sepulchre
Oil on canvas, 99 × 122 cm

A very suggestive example of how Bezzuoli translated his own knowledge of 16th and 17th-century painting into a modern style. The painting makes reference to the heroic landscape of the classicist tradition of Lorrain and Poussin, but accentuates the contrasting effects of light and shadow as required by the canons of the sublime romantic. Executed in about 1843, the work was admired for the harmonious consonance between the natural spectacle and the funereal epilogue to Christ's life, which was a way of recognising Bezzuoli's ability to merge the new naturalist poetics with his background as a pre-eminent historical painter.

Romantic painting of historical genre

"Finally the Venuses, Adonises, Cupids, Minervas, Psyches and Ganymides, the venerable and frightening beards of Jupiter and Pluto, all the mad and obscene adventures of mythology have been banished from sensible 19th-century painting." Thus wrote Defendente Sacchi in 1830 in celebration of the painting of Hayez representing the generous feats of medieval and renaissance heroes, facts of the fatherland's history that could foster new passions and new fancies in romantic man. This is precisely the idea of the progress of art that was embodied in the historical genre painting practised at the Academy for artists, such as the Sabatelli or Giuseppe Bezzuoli – artists who had in fact been formed during the crisis of neo-classicism. They were convinced that, in order to overcome the canons imposed by antiquated models, it was necessary, not only to invoke the themes of modern history, but to make them more attractive by reclaiming the grand pictorial examples of 16th and 17th-century Italian art, considered the most appropriate for expression of sublime concepts and 'natural' passions.

GIUSEPPE BEZZUOLI
Carlo VIII entering Florence
Oil on canvas, 290 × 356 cm

Commissioned by the grand duke in 1827, the painting was finished in 1829. The composition was inspired by the passage recounting the entrance of Carlo VIII into Florence to be found in the *Histories of the city of Florence* by Jacopo Nardi (1535). The painter however stoops to some rather pathetic suggestions – for example, in concealing the distress and anger of some of its personages – as well as to some rather cautious nationalist allusions – by placing at the painting's right the highest representatives of the opposition to imperial aims (Capponi, Savonarola, Baccio Valori and Macchiavelli). Received as the most beautiful creation "of

the modern Italians", the painting would constitute the fundamental point of reference for the nascent painting of historical genre, demonstrating how a careful study of 17th-century naturalism could contribute to rendering the principle of truth more flexible, and the expression of feelings, more touching.

FRANCESCO HAYEZ
The two Foscari
Oil on canvas,
121 × 167.5 cm

The painting was carried out in Milan around 1852 and acquired in 1854 by Andrea Maffei who donated it to the Royal Galleries of Florence in 1886. Its 'political' subject was taken from Daru's edition of the *History of the Venetian Republic* (1826). However, the figurative transposition of the subject, rich in tragic and pathetic elements, is due Byron's famous drama *The two Foscari*, which Hayez illustrates through recourse to scenographic expedients providing a spectacular result and an equally captivating painting style, with its noble references to the great Venetian tradition of the 16th Century.

AMOS CASSIOLI
The battle of Legnano
Oil on canvas, 370 × 640 cm

Cassioli entered this painting in the Ricasoli Competition decreed by the Provisional Government of Tuscany on September 23, 1859 under the section "historical paintings", which called for the execution of paintings depicting glorious episodes of ancient and modern Italian history. The painting was finished only at the end of 1870, receiving nevertheless great acclaim, even during its execution, from the panel of judges, who appreciated both the excellence of the histori-cal documentation and the novelty of the style, modernised in the grand manner of contemporary French painting without however omitting the 'truths' introduced into historical painting by the examples of the Neapolitan, Domenico Morelli, who was very highly esteemed in Tuscany.

ROOM 6

Inquiry into 'the real' between Florence and Naples

Just after mid-century, the romantic canons linked to the composition of historical painting were overcome and began to give way to impassioned inquiry, both cognitive and emotional, into the diverse aspects of Nature and the events of contemporary history – the first fertile domain of the debate conducted by the generation of macchiaioli *painters. In fact, around 1856 new ideas on the principle of truth and reality converged upon Florence, brought mainly by Domenico Morelli and Saverio Altamura, who just back from Paris, proclaimed the urgent need for experimentation outside the constricting limits of artistic genres. The works of Cabianca and Borrani serve as good examples of the transition from constrained art to the representation of reality through well-matched luminous contrasts: a compositional method which in these years was also common to the academic, Stefano Ussi, who uses it mainly in sketches and highly intimate portraits, as well as Giovanni Fattori, who in tackling the then fashionable themes of history, avoids commemorative tones thanks to an atmospheric painting, in poetic harmony with the anti-heroic mundanity of the topics dealt with.*

GIUSEPPE ABBATI

Cloister

Oil on cardboard,
19.3 × 25.2 cm

It is one of the works that Abbati, who arrived in Florence in late 1860, painted while directly involved with the artistic atmosphere of Caffè Michelangelo, especially the works of D'Ancona and Sernesi, aimed at the study of volume and light. In this regard, Diego Martelli wrote that the painter who practised in the cloisters of Santa Croce "where, as the monument was being restored at the time, many multi-coloured marble masses were produced, offering the observant student the advantages of finding himself before masses of very well-defined shapes, definite contrasts and almost elementary colours and chiaroscuro".

ODOARDO BORRANI

Middle Age

Oil on canvas,
145 × 121 cm

This painting, dated 1864, is a nostalgic return to Medieval Tuscany concentrated in an episode of a city feud with the sunlit hills of San Miniato in the background. Trained at the school of Gaetano Bianchi and, therefore, in the cult of fresco painting of the 14th and 15th Centuries, here

Borrani evokes a scene of the past – which in those years could find analogies in the pre-Raphaelite revivals – with figurative devices modernised according to the new vision of the 'macchia'. The work demonstrates how it was possible to bring about the union of avant-garde poetics with the noble academic tradition still represented by the historical painting of Giuseppe Bezzuoli.

VINCENZO CABIANCA
The Florentine storytellers
Oil on canvas, 76 × 100 cm

Displayed at the Italian Fair of 1861, where it was acquired by Vittorio Emanuele II, the painting, romantic only in part, evokes the most nostalgic and lyrical aspects of medieval civilisation. Although approximating the canons of historical genre in the choice of topic and some of its formal as-

pects, this work by Cabianca, dated 1861, in fact reveals clear evidence of his experimentation with colour and light that demonstrates a direct knowledge of the results simultaneously attained by the Neapolitans (mainly Morelli and Altamura) in the study and rendering of truth, thus acquiring representational autonomy from the ethical and didactic values of the art of romanticism.

Room 7

Antonio Ciseri and the commemorative portrait

When Antonio Ciseri organised a exhibit of the portraits from his study on Via delle Belle Donne in 1871, the number of visitors was such that entrance to the show had to be temporarily suspended in order to avoid dangerous overcrowding – an obvious indication of the fame enjoyed by the artist, especially in official cultural circles. Ciseri championed the primacy of design and form, that while excluding spontaneous naturalism, adhered to reality, appealing, like the French after Ingres, to the rigorous devices of analogy. Renowned for his ability to fix physiognomy in drawing, Ciseri's portraits instead resort to rendition through synthetic structures and the slow and meticulous study of form and figure, which is normally made to stand out from an abstract background – a true plane of pose – thus avoiding distraction from the focus on the physiology and temperament of the personage depicted. These qualities of style and introspection earned the artist important commissions and made him the unquestioned master of the official or commemorative portrait, in antithesis to the naturalistic studies of the latter half of the 19th Century.

Antonio Ciseri
Portrait of Giovanni Dupré
Oil on canvas, 67 × 54 cm

The Florentine Galleries commissioned the painting, completed in 1885, to Ciseri for the portrait collection of the Uffizi shortly after the death of the famous sculptor (1882). A copy of the portrait carried out for the Dupré family in 1868, the painting reveals Ciseri's exceptional abilities in portraiture, able to unify as a whole the observation of the real – often filtered through the use of new 'photographic' techniques – with coherent control of form, sustained by the imposing drawing that had its origins in the models of Ingres and his French pupils.

RAFFAELLO SORBI
Portrait of the sculptor Emilio Zocchi
Oil on canvas, 51.5 × 39 cm

Dedicated to his sculptor friend, in 1868 Sorbi signed this portrait demonstrating the influence that the teachings of Ciseri still had on the young painter. It also illustrates his going beyond the maestro's formal abstraction in favour of a more direct expression of feelings. These are the years when Florence sees animated discussion of the topics of truth and the need to overcome academic canons through experimentation of new techniques of vision. These are the years that mark the first important stages of Sorbi's career, directed mainly toward historical genre painting, but also able to depict fresh 'snapshots', which were to be admired by Telemaco Signorini, amongst others.

BALLROOM

Part of the quarters called the "Bourbon" or the "New Palatine" the Ballroom was designed by Pasquale Poccianti around 1825, though never fully brought to completion, as can be surmised by observing the incomplete ornamental particulars of the roof. Today it contains a group of statues by Aristodemo Costoli, Giovanni Dupré, Odoardo Fantacchiotti and Pio Fedi, forming a sculptural coterie of the first half of the 19th Century in Tuscany.

PIO FEDI
Saint Sebastian
Plaster, h. 165 cm

Sent from Rome as an entry in the contest for the *pensionato artistico*, it was exhibited in the Academy of Florence in 1844, where it commanded a certain amount of attention on the part of critics for the unexpected synthesis of classical and renaissance references and the modern sensibility of its depiction of reality. The favourable reception of the work, fostered by contemporary attention to the naturalistic trends in art determining the surpassing of the purist culture in which the same Fedi had been formed, occasioned several commissions for the sculptor, amongst which the important duty of realising the statues of Nicola Pisano and Andrea Cesalpino for the loggia of the Uffizi.

GIOVANNI DUPRÉ
Bacchus of the cryptogam
Marble, h. 115 cm

Acquired by the State in 1974, along with the *Feasting Bacchus* – both from the Mylius palace, later The Rochefoucault of Genova – this marble work is dated 1859 and shows the interest of the Sienese sculptor in the theories which, in France and in the wake of Théophile Gautier, advocated the use of past figurative traditions to carry out evocative and sensual functions. On the other hand, the idea of the work itself had matured through contact with the ancient treasures of Herculano and Pompeii, admired by Dupré during his stay in Naples, financed by the Tuscan grand duke, and reinterpreted here as an elegant formal means for representing a modern allegory.

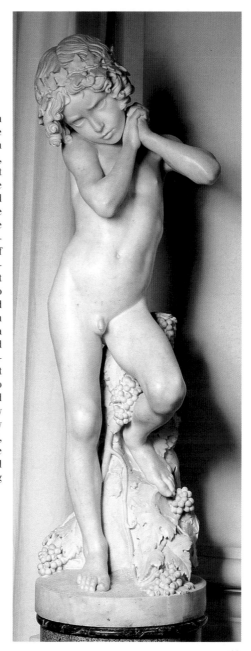

Room 8

Portraits of the era of Florence the capital

The graceful posture of many of the portraits painted after the second half of the 19th Century points out how, beginning in the 60s, even portraiture responded to the appeal of the renewing influences coming mainly from France. The refined formal balance that purist art had established in order to portray the moderation and civility of the main characters of the bourgeois restoration is shaken by the emergence of more direct feelings that infuse the portrait with the attributes of a 'snapshot'. The artist now captures and fixes as absolutes the gestures and expressions of a particularly charming biography. Thus, in the post-unification years, the formal austerity of Antonio Ciseri's commemorative portraits coexists with the sensitive sprightliness of the noblewoman Morrocchi di Puccinelli, with Cassioli's allusions to the portraiture of Degas, and with the solemn humanity of Giovanni Fattori's portraits – all indications of the experience of similar aesthetic adventures, in a manner of speaking, outside the atelier.

Giovanni Fattori
Self-portrait
Oil on canvas, 59 × 47 cm

Executed in 1854, the painting was acquired in 1951 for the Uffizi collection of self-portraits. It represents an important stage in Fattori's early artistic formation, still marked by the style of his teacher, Giuseppe Bezzuoli, and by the years spent in the Academy of Florence studying both ancient and modern art. He was however already on the road to chromatic and formal experimentation that is to anticipate the imminent exercises of the *macchiaioli* on reality and how character and particularities of physiognomy are captured in painting without mediation, all with the purpose of seizing the truest identity.

ANTONIO PUCCINELLI
Portrait of the noblewoman Morrocchi
Oil on canvas, 104 × 86 cm

This portrait, from between 1855 and 1860, is the maximum expression of the 'Ingres School', initiated by Luigi Mussini in mid-century and then carried on by Luigi Pollastrini and Antonio Ciseri, converting it into the most modern trend of Tuscan painting just prior to the advent of the *macchiaioli*. The portrait reveals in both its execution and accomplished form, what Ingres had adopted to idealise the main personages of France in the time of Napoleon III – the way to arrive at a renewal of academic canons, affording unexpected perspectives even to the portraits of aristocrats and high bourgeois.

ROOM 9

The landscape schools of the mid-19th Century: traditional aspects and the Barbizon influence

During the first months of 1856, one of the most heatedly debated topics in the meetings at Caffè Michelangelo was that of landscape painting, a topic brought to the forefront by the enthusiastic narrations of Stefano De Tivoli and Altamura who, fresh from their Paris visit, mysteriously alluded to the ton gris *adopted by French landscapers and the use of the black mirror which, by eliminating intermediates colours, allowed the artist to capture light and shadow, that is to say, the* chiaroscuro, *in its entirety, through the* macchia. *The immediate adherence of these painters to the poetics of Barbizon came to influence the first exercises* en plein air *of the so-called school of Staggia, that is, the same environment in which De Tivoli, Carlo and Andrea Markò had overcome the excitement of romantic landscape – still living on in the paintings of Fontanesi – for the sake of a more analytical naturalism, definitively freed from 17th-century models and other characteristic conventions of the genre.*

ANTONIO FONTANESI
After the rain
Oil on canvas, 128 × 192 cm

The painting, which won the medal of the Royal Commission at the 1861 Italian World Fair, was acquired by the king for two thousand six-hundred liras, thus becoming part of the dynastic collections of Pitti Palace and thereafter, the Modern Art Gallery. Together with the *Countryside with grazing flock*, also part of the royal collection, this large panorama represents, in contrast with the more lucid and abstract Tuscan vision, an example of landscape painting still strongly permeated by romantic feeling. It is nonetheless quite interesting because of the variety of atmospheric effects whose study was at the core of the ongoing reform of landscape painting in those years.

SERAFINO DE TIVOLI
A pasture
Oil on canvas, 102 × 73 cm

Exhibited in the Florentine Promotrice of 1859, it is one of the few paintings from this period remaining to us. It is the period that best docu-

ments De Tivoli's efforts to integrate his Parisian experiences with the Tuscan landscape tradition, which received much of its initial impetus from De Tivoli, together with the Markò brothers, Gelati and Ademollo. What im-

presses even more is the atmospheric effect and the simplicity of the topic, interpreted as a "piece of reality seen from the window" that is to say, described in same way that Martelli would read the paintings of the impressionists.

Not There

Luigi Catani, Alfonso King of Leon discusses the World System with Hebrew astronomers.

ROOM 10

The Cristiano Banti collection

The collection has been in the possession of the Gallery since 1958, after having been bequeathed to Adriana Banti Ghiglia in 1955. It reflects the double personality of its original owner, a painter at first caught up by the French messages of Altamura, Morelli and De Tivoli, but also amateur and patron of unconventional tastes. The painter's works show preferences for the creations of the Roman, Nino Costa, as well as Fontanesi and, more generally, the naturalism of Corot and painters of Barbizon, re-read in light of a more cultured and formally mediated painting, able to introduce rural-life painting to those genres most often commissioned at the request of the bourgeois. The collector's paintings, however, recall to us the grand and cosmopolitanism home of Banti where, amongst others, Boldini would work, comfortably responding to the dictates of the atmosphere with the chic elegance of his portraits.

CRISTIANO BANTI

*The wood-
gathering women
(The plunderers)*

Oil on canvas,
62.5 × 135.5 cm

The painting can be dated to around 1881 on the basis of a written testimony by Cecioni that surfaced in 1884 and describes the singular topic represented here. These asocial women were frequent in the fields of the Maremma, where they would go, dressed in colourful rags for clothing, to pilfer and poach, thus the epithets, 'plunderer' or 'wrong-doer'.

Several sketches by Banti exist on the subject, all designed with the same diagonal arrangement of the scene and furious painting style – almost as an analogy to the theme – that mark this artist's stylistic and conceptual distance from Fattori and his vision of the Maremma swampland, more formally austere and less prone to narrative suggestion.

GIOVANNI BOLDINI
Portrait of Alaide Banti

Oil on wood-plate,
42.5 × 23 cm

This is one of the numerous portraits of Alaide (here at about the age of twelve) which Boldini painted in Tuscany, feeling the attraction of the elegant climate of Banti's home where he stayed as a guest during his years in Florence (1862-1869). There was even a romance between the painter, already mature and established in Paris, and Banti's daughter. However, the marriage plans were unexpectedly interrupted, leaving the young girl heartbroken. Of all of Boldini's portraits present in the collection, this is without a doubt the most famous and most suitable to documenting the style that he shared with the *macchiaioli.*

FRANCESCO SAVERIO ALTAMURA
Profile of a woman
Oil on canvas, 39 × 29 cm

Carried out four years after the painter's arrival in Florence, that is to say in 1852, this portrait likely represents his first wife, Elena, a painter of Greek origin, who he first met in the revolutionary atmosphere of Naples before 1848 and then again in Florence in 1852. In fact, the style of the work coincides with Altamura's Florentine paintings, in which the prevailing a naturalism is still contained within the rigorous execution.

ROOM 11 *see caricature*

The Diego Martelli collection

The painting collection of Diego Martelli, bequeathed to the city council of Florence in 1897, is tangible testimony to the aesthetic trends of the macchiaioli's *most attentive interpreter and was born of the affectionate intermingling of friendship, enthusiasm and polemics. The wood-plates of Abbati and Sernesi, the collector-critic's favourites, are along the lines of the works of the 'allied' southerners, Grita and Tedesco, and the sketches of Fattori and Lega, painted for the most part in Castiglioncello, where the hospitality of the Martelli family provided these artists with a tranquil and protracted relationship with nature and the opportunity to share their experiences. The echoes of the discussions in Caffè Michelangelo can be sensed in their preference for outdoor painting from life and the information on French art, to which refer the paintings of Camille Pissarro, acquired by Martelli at the time when the impressionists were subjected to unfortunate critical drubbing, as well as in the evident naturalistic inclinations of the works of Zandomeneghi and Cecioni, that recall the patient pedagogy of Martelli, committed to explaining to his doubtful and reluctant friends that in the greyness of the expositions, impressionist painting represented 'the window', because it was here that the light dominated.*

SALVATORE GRITA
The vow against nature
Plaster, h. 65.5 cm

Executed in Florence between 1860 and 1870, this is one of the very few known works of the Sicilian sculptor Salvatore Grita, who arrived in Tuscany during the time of the Risorgimento and was a friend of Martelli and the *macchiaioli*, as well as co-editor with them of the "Gazzetino delle arti del disegno". Later Gritas progressively reduced his sculpting in order to follow his vocation as socialist-leaning polemicist, already implied in this work denouncing the drama of forced ordinations, in a crude, expressive style, comparable to certain pages of the nascent realistic literature.

FEDERICO ZANDOMENEGHI

In bed

Oil on canvas,
60.5 × 73.5 cm

The painting was probably made during the same years that Diego Martelli was in Paris (1878-1879), that is, when the Florentine polemicist began his friendly relationships with Monet, Degas, Pissarro and Zola, sending their articles to several Italian newspapers to inform of the novelties emerging from the impressionist school. A fundamental chronicle of the contribution of French naturalism to the ongoing controversy on truth, the painting introduces to the intimist genre practised by the *macchiaioli* a note of great expressive freedom, fed by the literary topics and open-mindedness that many Italians had learned, during their stays Paris, to translate into luminous and evocative painting.

CAMILLE PISSARRO
Landscape (The storm's approach)
Oil on canvas, 60×74 cm

Pissarro gave this painting, together with another present in the collection, to Martelli so that he would exhibit it in the Florentine Promotrice of 1878. Neither of the paintings was sold, and both were severely criticised by the public and Florentine artists, who could not conceive of painting without a recognisable pictorial and formal design. However, Diego Martelli defended the two paintings, which remained in his collection as manifestos of impressionist painting in Italy, of which the critic was one of the most adamant champions. In fact, he considered it to be absolutely necessary to overcome the reticence of the Academy by admitting French innovation in colour and atmosphere.

SILVESTRO LEGA
A walk in the garden
Oil on canvas, 35×22.5 cm

Possibly the same painting that Lega presented at the 1870 National Exhibition of Parma under the title *Walk*, this painting represents a high-level expression of the spirit and style that distinguishes the Piagentina years, when the observation of truth, reserved to the cultivated and consoling aspects of the countryside near Florence, was translated into clear and composed volumes caressed by a light that is at once natural and abstracting, aiming to accentuate the constructive values of the 'macchia' applied to subjects with strong emotional content.

FEDERICO ZANDOMENEGHI

Honeymoon (Fishing on the Seine)

Oil on wood-plate, 16×29 cm

Martelli sent this painting to Florence, together with two paintings by Pissarro, some dry points by Desboutin and another work of Zandomeneghi, *In bed*, in order to inform the Tuscan public of the most advanced innovations emerging from Paris. Exhibited in the Promotrice of 1878 under the title *Honeymoon*, it caused a sensation for its innovative compositional arrangement and colour, considered to be strident and unreal. However, it demonstrated the painter's knowledge of the aesthetic concepts of Impressionism and what Martelli hoped would be performed in order to renew art.

The theme of genre from the end of the grand duchy to unification

The fervent Florentine discussions of the 1850s on the new ways of conceptualising painting, especially that of landscape, did not compromise the public and private fortunes of the other genre subjects. Historical themes, for example, unfettered by their traditional duties of civil education, gave rise to free and airy compositions, in which the philology of history was subordinated to the studied proportions of light and colour. Fragments of contemporary life also survived, receiving numerous commissions in mid-century, including above all the tearful and edifying paintings of Domenico Induno and the conversational scenes represented here in the paintings of Silvestro Lega and Pietro Saltini. The works of Cecioni were counterposed to these in several ways – these same soothing topics were rendered grotesque and tragic by his introducing the restlessness of the post-unification era into the affective conventions of the Restoration.

Never found this

SILVESTRO LEGA
The starling's song
Oil on canvas, 158 × 98 cm

Exhibited for the first time in the Florentine Promotrice of 1867, from the outset the painting received notable acclaim from critics, who judged it one of the greatest achievements of the artist, who had reached his full creative maturity. The striking feature of the work is the description of the domestic episode which here is nearly transfigured by the sustained formal character, evidently inspired by 15th-century Tuscan painting, mainly that of Piero della Francesca.

The painting dates back to the time of Piagentina, and the woman playing the piano is Virginia Batelli, sentimentally linked to the painter, in a moment of happy activity – in fact, one of the favourite pastimes of the woman and her hospitable family, whose villa was located in a picturesque locale in the immediate vicinity of Florence.

DOMENICO INDUNO
The antique dealer
Oil on canvas, 81 × 55 cm

The painting comes from the collections of the Academy, where it has been documented since 1888. It represents an interesting aspect of the genre painting practised in Lombardy, a genre dependent upon the educational and moral requirements consequent to public viewing – in antithesis to the abstract vocation of the Tuscans – and, therefore, prone to the illustration and study of emotions. Publicly acclaimed, Induno participates in numerous and important exhibitions, where he earns both awards and recognition, thanks precisely to his specialisation in the subject of the genre, very much to the tastes and demand of the current bourgeois.

ROOM 13

The patriotic theme with democratic overtones

The need for a wide-spread, yet controlled dissemination of the facts occurring on the eve of Italian independence, suggested to the 1859 provisional Government the idea of holding a competition in several categories of art works. The entries were to commemorate the recomposing, under the protection of the Savoy monarchy, of a conflict that had occasioned new myths and new heroes for Italy to celebrate. So, the propaganda and hagiographic side of the undertaking saw the creation of exemplary and moving figurative episodes, while the democratic motives of some of the new generation of artists focused their attentions on minor episodes of the newly added chapters in Italy's history, those deemed the most touching in their revelations to oppressed and suffering mankind. A masterpiece of this poetic understanding of the fate of the 'vanquished' is Magenta by Fattori, around which are centred the military paintings by Lega and other artists that addressed patriotic issues with their minds on the actuality of the story and their willing hearts on resolving the drama and pain through the harmonious beauty of nature.

GIOVANNI FATTORI

The Italian camp after the battle of Magenta

Oil on canvas, 232 × 348 cm

Commissioned on the occasion of the Ricasoli competition of 1859 in the category of "battle paintings" (Curtatone, Palestro, Magenta and San Martino) commemorating the second war of independence, the painting was presented, still incomplete, at the 1861 Italian Fair in Flo-

rence, and later at the Florentine Promotrice of 1862. It is the first painting of the modern historical genre, in that it unifies attentive documentation of the attire and weapons through naturalistic observations translated in a controlled range of complementary colours – composed according to the canons of *macchiaioli* painting – and pathetic notations, by now participants in the imminent culture of Verismo.

ALESSANDRO LANFREDINI

The Italian recruits of the Sigmund Regiment after the battle of Magenta.
Oil on canvas, 173×232 cm

Like the painting by Fattori, this was entered in the Ricasoli competition of 1859 in the section "military episodes of the last war". It was presented incomplete at the 1861 Italian Fair in Florence, and nonetheless earned the artist a medal for the narrative efficacy of the composi-tion and its brilliant ex-ecution in the purist tra-dition. The episode de-scribes the moment in which, after the battle of Magenta, it was discov-ered that the cartridge holders of some Italian conscripts in the Austri-an Regiment, found dead on the field of bat-tle, had been emptied of their projectiles by the recruits themselves in order to not kill their countrymen of the Franco-Italian troops.

Historical genres to the forefront of the exhibitions

The experimental tensions that arose from the meetings in Caffè Michelangelo necessarily had to come to terms with the vital tradition of Tuscan academic art of the latter half of the century. The presentation at the exhibitions of many works of unquestionable quality based on recovering the techniques and form of past masters and French contemporaries, frequently caused young artists to doubt the much-debated suitability of reproducing truth while avoiding the exhausting practice of the atelier. *The extraordinary capacity to merge observations of reality with the intellectual contributions of literary mediation, most evident in the works of Antonio Ciseri and, with the added aspects of a more captivating narration, those of Gabriele Castagnola and Rodolfo Morgari, constituted therefore a kind of formal counterpoint to the evolution of* macchiaioli *art, which placed experimentation of a renewed vision of nature before the frigid abstraction of academic subjects.*

ANTONIO CISERI
Ecce Homo
Oil on canvas, 380 × 292 cm

Exhibited for the first time in Ciseri's study shortly after his death, the large painting received overt acclaim even from the anti-academic Diego Martelli, who immediately praised its luminance and the transparency effects of the whites in the scene's background. The painting required from the artist a long period of work that would bear fruit in 1891, that is, when the formalist rigor of official painting had already begun to

La Monàca Buti

find profitable correspondence in similar trends in European art. It was then that Ciseri as well would be able to appropriate the literary elements of French painting – from the 'Romaness' of Gerôme to the positivist Christianity of Renan – and the aesthetic elements of the classicism of Alma Tadema.

GABRIELE CASTAGNOLA
The episode of Filippo Lippi and the Nun Buti
Oil on canvas, 223 × 159 cm

The painting represents one of the most cordial aspects of the historical genre painting, illustrating the legendary episode in the life of Filippo Lippi within a narrative vein sustained by the masterful drawing and fanciful imagination that the painter exploits to evoke a fabulous and captivating renaissance, rather than the ethical and exemplary one preferred by the historical painting of romanticism. Castagnola moved from Genova to Florence in the crucial years of the Caffè Michelangelo, immediately affirming himself as a skilled narrator of historical episodes that were both picturesque and appropriate to transposing present-day customs and feelings onto an age-old story.

printed in reverse

La Sorella Maggiore
Cane che Salva

Stefano Ussi and the climate of the World Fairs

The success attained with The expulsion of the Duke of Athens *at the Italian Fair of 1861 demonstrated that the topic of ancient history continued to be a privileged field of formal experimentation – more appreciated, in fact, than the contemporary themes which some dissenting artists were trying to bring to the forefront in those years. Diego Martelli wrote openly of their divergence, criticising the official exhibition establishment which, opposed to the new, was celebrating the rhetoric of contents. Actually, Ussi's painting, as well as* Buonconte *by Smargiassi, represented the evolutionary summit of historical painting of the Romantic tradition of Domenico Morelli, committed as they were to strict narration of events arising from the definition of solid masses revealed and counterpoised by the strong chiaroscuro, or to the prevalence of naturalist scenes painted as representations of the real.*

STEFANO USSI *cacciata*
The expulsion of the Duke of Athens
Oil on canvas, 320 × 452 cm

Begun in Rome, where Ussi had been awarded a *pensionato artistico*, the painting was concluded in Florence in 1861 and presented at the national exhibition of that year, attaining notable success and the winning first prize. The topic of the painting comes from Machiavelli's *Istorie Florentine* and *The Duke of Athens* by Tommaseo, and represents Gualtieri di Brienne's indecision in signing his resignation from the *Signoria* of Florence. In spite of Martelli's protests, which accused the exhibition's jury of favouring the Academy, the painting marked the transcending of the historical romantic genre and demonstrated the painter's knowledge of the realism introduced in Florence by Domenico Morelli.

51

GABRIELE SMARGIASSI

*Buonconte di
Montefeltro killed
in battle*

Oil on canvas, 213 × 300 cm

The success of this work at the Italian Fair of 1861 convinced the king to buy it for his own collection, paying the highest price ever for a painting. As Salvatore di Giacomo wrote, underlining the prevalence of literary aspects in historical genre painting and, at the same time, the effect obtained by the broad atmosphere and paling colours of the scene: "Smargiassi wanted his characters to express something through a meditated, somewhat romantic and historical composition: he wanted them to nearly hover, as Dantesque spirits, the unearthly figures of saints or the heroic figures of Ariosto and Tasso".

The celebration of the post-unification Risorgimento: the rebirth of the applied arts

It was the opinion of Demetrio Carlo Finocchietti, enterprising administrator of the Savoy court at Pitti Palace, that in order to consolidate the bonds of fraternity forged on the battlefield, nothing else remained but to "measure oneself in the arena of industry", thus providing incentive to the tastes and creativity, not only of artists, but of the most disparate categories of artisans as well, who would find the national and international exhibitions to be the most appropriate forums for comparisons and emulation. It was certainly in keeping with these precepts that Vittorio Emanuele II proceeded to acquire paintings and decorations destined for the palace – which was thus transformed into the official gallery of the modern Italian style – though he also commissioned works that were to attest, in their content and formal conquests, to the creative vitality springing from the travails of the Risorgimento. The result was a weave of a multiplicity of aspirations and styles that, on behalf of the sought-for and accepted plurality, could enumerate the masterpieces of the avant-garde artists and works of the hagiographic Savoys – works admirable for the techniques employed, as well as their ability to achieve bold eclecticism.

ALESSANDRO
MONTENERI,
GUGLIELMO CIANI,
DOMENICO BRUSCHI
*Decorated cabinet
for the Italian
crown*
Mahogany marquetry with
maple and mother-of-
pearl, h. 327 cm

Begun in 1860 by the Perugian sculptor and marquetry master, Alessandro Monteneri, after the design of Bruschi and structural plan by Ciani, the cabinet was presented at the Italian Fair of 1861, as well as that in London in 1862. The Municipality of Perugia donated it to the king, who immediately placed it in Pitti Palace in order to demonstrate that the neo-renais- sance style, accompa- nied by the refined readopting of ancient techniques, was valued and accorded the highest levels, also for its implicit social and politics values.

VINCENZO GEMITO
Portrait of Giuseppe Verdi

Bronze, h. 50 cm
§

We know that Giuseppe Verdi, giving in to the entreaties of Domenico Morelli, commissioned Gemito with his portrait when he was in Naples for the performances of *Don Carlos* and *Aida*.

Verdi was a guest at the Crocelle Hotel, where the sculptor came to stay for the few days necessary to model the bust, experiencing not little indecision regarding the 'cut' to adopt in the portrait of the renowned musician. He would finish it in 1873, achieving noteworthy efficacy also in the im-

pressionist rendering of the subsequent bronze cast of the plaster model. The original was placed in the Rest Home for musicians in Milan and later reproduced by the sculptor in many copies such as this one, which has been in the Gallery collection since 1927.

Portraits from the era of Umberto I

Italy's annexation of Rome (1870), and the transfer of the realm's capital there from Florence (1871) are the events that close, also in a symbolic sense, the period of the Risorgimento, thereby opening the long and arduous stage of building the unified state, a difficult undertaking, given the multitude of problems inherited from centuries of backwardness. The Progressivism of the Risorgimento, which had fostered the formal experiments of the macchiaioli in art, now gives way to a social conservatism, armed against the earliest insubordination of the subaltern classes, upheld by the aristocracy and bourgeoisie entrepreneurs. Celebration of the new protagonists, depicted in the luxury of officialdom or the comfortable peace of suburban villas, will be the task of artists such as Vittorio Corcos and Michele Gordigiani, who are careful to depict these men and women in a clear, very well-defined painting style, after the French example of the salon paintings – far indeed from the austere formalism that characterised the intimist preferences of the macchiaioli.

Victor Hug

MICHELE GORDIGIANI
*Portrait of the
painter's wife,
Gabriella Coujère*
Oil on canvas, 72 × 58 cm

Towards the century's
end, Gordigiani was
considered one of Italy's
most important por-
trait-artists for his ability to harmonise acade-
mic tradition with the
innovation of European
figurative culture, espe-
cially that of France. His
mastery is evident in
this elegant portrait of
his wife, captured in the
almost blinding reflec-
tion of the noonday
light. The fame of the
painter increased sig-
nificantly in 1861, when
he painted a portrait of
Vittorio Emanuele II,
and immediately there-
after one of the queen,
as well as other royalty
from France and Eng-
land.

VITTORIO CORCOS
*The daughter of
Jack la Bolina*
Oil on canvas, 139 × 105 cm

Dated to around 1888, this portrait represents a example of the mundane style of Corcos, characterised by well-defined painting, after the example of French models from Carolus Duran to the impressionists, and aimed at exalting the new pomp of the high bourgeoisie entrepreneurs, often with strong literary implications. It is evident how the elegant nonchalance of the style is combined here with his ability to narrate almost the character's history, in its intimate sentimental mystery. It was such compositional aspects that earned Corcos extraordinary success at exhibitions, as well as the appellative: *peintre des jolies femmes.*

Sala 18

The municipal inventory of the years 1912-1925 (*macchiaioli* and other schools)

The figurative journey that this room presents – bringing together works from the municipal store dating back to the years when the convention between the State and the Florence City Council was still in force – allows assessing the analogies and differences that link or distinguish the main personages of the time of the macchiaioli. *It is a rich repertoire, whose highlights include some of the greatest achievements of Fattori and Signorini. The small studies of Vito D'Ancona, full of luminous matter, and the poetic analogies of form and colour studied directly on reality by Abbati, Sernesi and Borrani, constitute a visual and theoretical counterpoint to the independent evolution of the art of Fattori. It is a journey from the first* macchiaioli, *the pioneers of 1859, through the happy experiences in Leghorn and Castiglioncello, and up to the style of the last years when the most modern current within the movement, of which Signorini is the most international expression, dictates the dominance of sign over colour.*

GIOVANNI FATTORI
The Palmieri rotunda
Oil on wood-plate,
12 × 35 cm

Painted in 1866, the plate represents some ladies resting at the rotunda of the well-known Leghorn bath houses, from which extends the luminous horizon, accented by the strong contrast of the shady area in the foreground, thus achieving the effect of a wide-open horizon, nonetheless contained within the reduced dimensions of the painting. This work is often cited as one of Fattori's greatest masterpieces, not only for its fresh immediacy and the attentive studiousness of its chromatic couplings, based on the principles of complementarity, but also for its compositional cut, attested to by his pictorial meditations during that summer of 1866, as well as a notebook full of preparatory drawings documenting the gradual steps leading from the study of reality to its rendering in the *atelier*.

GIOVANNI FATTORI

La libecciata (The Southwesterly Gale)

Oil on wood-plate, 28.5 × 68 cm

One of Fattori's most famous paintings, *La libecciata* expresses with great efficacy the poetics of the artist's last period, very different from that of the more idyllic and lyrical decade 1870-80. In fact, in describing the conflict of the elements of nature, Fattori paints a restless metaphor of his own existential condition, creating an image very akin to the symbolist naturalism of the contemporary poetry of Giovanni Pascoli and an idea of landscape seemingly abbreviated, but well suited to expressing a touching concept through almost sensory painting.

GIOVANNI FATTORI
The stirrup
Oil on canvas, 90 × 130 cm

When exhibited in Florence in 1880 it was interpreted as one of the apices of naturalistic aesthetics for the manner in which Fattori had succeeded in communicating the clear impression of the 'real', balancing parts defined by the drawing with others hardly outlined and thus amenable to rendering the tragic dynamism of the scene. It was Renato Fucini who suggested the theme to Fattori, while the artist was working on another subject, *The explosion of the chest*, equally set at an oblique view and the immediate rendering of a moving and spectacular event: images that well suited the sensibility of the artist in his old age.

TELEMACO SIGNORINI
Penitentiary of Portoferraio
Oil on canvas, 56 × 80 cm

Carried out in 1894, it was presented the following year at the Florentine Promotrice and again in 1901 at the 8th Biennial of Venice. Together with the *Room of the anxious* and *The morning's awakening*, it represents the moment when Signorini

began his adherence to those aspects of French naturalism which, in Italy, would unite in the literary and figurative poetics of social veris-

mo. The idea of the painting came to Signorini after visiting the penitentiary during his first trip to Elba in 1888, and reveals in the artist an expressive charge clearly comparable with similar experiences in Mitteleurope.

TELEMACO SIGNORINI
Roofs at Riomaggiore
Oil on canvas, 79 × 55 cm

The painting depicts a view from above the town of Riomaggiore illuminated by blue-grey tones that highlight, in the absence of more de-

cisive chromatic contrasts, the painting's drawing and perspective structure. Part of a series on the maritime village (1881-1897), it represents a visual counterpoint to the book *Riomaggiore*, written and illustrated by the selfsame Signorini.

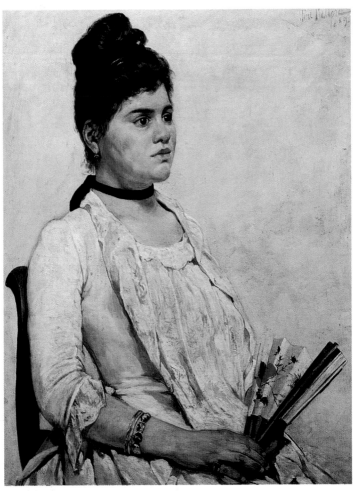

GIOVANNI FATTORI

*Portrait of his
stepdaughter*

Oil on canvas, 71 × 55 cm

The youth depicted here is Giulia Marinelli, daughter of Marianna Bigazzi, who would wed Fattori as her second husband in 1891, the same year in which Giulia would also marry the Uruguayan, Domingo Laporte. It is commonly held that the painting represents an apex in the history of 19th-century portraiture, as much for its solid compositional idea, supported by the essentiality of the chromatic range and studied counterpoint of the tones, as for the psychological rendering of the youth, captured in the fixity of her pose, yet transmitting her physiological features, which the artist observes with lucid objectivity and subtle introspection.

The Ambron collection (*macchiaioli* and other schools)

This room, like the preceding one, contains fundamental works of the macchiaioli and other particularly note-worthy Italian artists belonging to the schools of both the North and South, which thus provide a meaningful panorama of art in the latter half of the 19th Century. With paintings from the municipal inventory, this collection underscores the early recognition and consequent appreciation of the art of the macchiaioli *in both the public and private spheres, each of which offers a fertile terrain for observations of the personalities within the movement, centred mainly in sketches and scribblings of the* macchia, *and the state of Art in post-unification Tuscany. It therefore provides the ideal occasion to visually summarise the time of the* macchiaioli – *parallel in its development to other important national experiences – from the years in Florence hosted a unitary and progressive movement caught up in the debate on 'truth', 'reality' and 'nature', on the heels of the discoveries of Piagentina and Castiglioncello, up to 1870, after which the personal styles of Fattori, Lega and Signorini emerge, outstanding, from the premises of the group.*

GIOVANNI FATTORI
Cousin Argia
Oil on cardboard,
36.2 × 29 cm

The portrait, chronologically the first of the artist's masterpieces in this genre, dates back to the early 1860s, when the painter spent long periods in Leghorn so that his wife, who suffered from tuberculosis, could benefit from the curative effects of the sea air. It is here, in fact, during the time spent with his family that Fattori develops an interest in portraiture, painting his cousin Argia with a fineness and introspection that recall the paintings of the Roman, Nino Costa and, through him, the enthralling vivacity of the portraits of Camille Corot.

ADRIANO CECIONI

Suicidal

Plaster, h. 217 cm

Modelled by Cecioni in Naples between 1865 and 1867 as the last work in his *pensionato artistico* from the Florentine Academy, the sculpture was acquired in 1891 by the Minister of Education, Pasquale Villari, for the Gallery of the Academy and transferred to Pitti Palace in 1924. The representation of the theme of suicide was judged to be immoral by the Florentine academe, which did not consider it worthy to be transferred to marble. On the other hand, it was very well received by defenders of verism in art, who extolled the innovation of the subject, the raw drama of the figure and, at the same time, the audacity of the allusion in the figure's pose to the ancient model of the orator.

ANTONIO MANCINI

Self-portrait in his study

Oil on wood-plate, 21.5 × 31.5 cm

This intense self-portrait set in the artist's colourful study, full of moulds and models, was likely executed between 1875 and 1878, as evinced by the artist's youthful appearance and the analogies to another *self-portrait* dated 1878. The extremely original composition and strong pathos of the

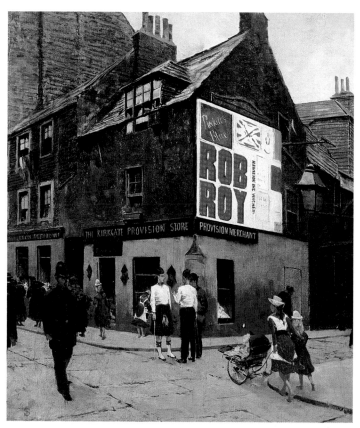

protagonist, indicate its having been made after Mancini's experiences in Paris, where the painter was involved with the artistic atmosphere surrounding the merchant Goupil; but they also foretell of the artist's growing hypochondria and the psychic alterations that henceforth would determine the introduction of eccentric formal solutions into his works.

Telemaco Signorini
Leith

Oil on canvas, 45 × 41. 5 cm

This worked was probably painted around 1881 when Signorini was staying in Edinburgh and travelled to Leith several times, as testified to by a diary from those times. During his stay in Great Britain the painter develops a more synthetic and abstract, than impressionist style, as can be evinced from the painting's composition, concentrated wholly on the geometric and chromatic manifestations of the billboard and the curtailed dynamism with which the passersby's figures are described.

ROOM 20

Campestral painting

After 1870, a second generation of macchiaioli *painters begins to affirm itself. Formed in direct contact with the movement's origins, they however took little time in separating themselves from the compositional measure of their maestri in order to follow the European aesthetics so wide-spread towards the end of the century. Amongst these artists, two major 'dynasties' emerge: that of the Gioli, linked to Fattori, and that of the Tommasi, influenced by Lega, who frequently spent time with them in the home of Bellariva. The occasion for their official debut was the 1886 exhibition in Leghorn, whose strongpoint was precisely this 'generation in between' composed of Ferroni, Francesco Gioli, Cannicci, Adolfo and Angiolo Tommasi, Cecconi and Panerai who in their studies from life in small format, common in these years also in the Roman and southern ambience, were already beginning to reveal their knowledge of the paintings of country-life presented in the Parisian* salons *by Jules Breton and Julien Bastien-Lepage.*

EGISTO FERRONI
At the fountain
Oil on canvas, 275 × 165 cm

Displayed in 1879 at the National Exhibition of Turin and the Florentine Promotrice the following year, the work was not appreciated by the juries, but was defended with great determination by the *macchiaioli* and Diego Martelli, who saw the large painting, formally ennobling topics that had until then been circumscribed within the domestic measure of genre painting, as Ferroni's keeping up with the monumental style of the paintings of campestral life being presented in contemporary Parisian *salons* by Jules Breton and Julien Bastien-Lepage.

TELEMACO SIGNORINI
September morning in Settignano
Oil on canvas, 58.5 × 64 cm

The painting is probably *The Scheggi tavern in Settignano* exhibited at the Promotrice of Florence in 1891, which was acquired by Umberto I. Carried out between 1883 and 1890, the years in which Signorini works assiduously in the hills of Settignano, frequenting the tavern for two months in the summer of 1885, the painting is one of the most moving visions of the Tuscan painter's late work. The result obtained is one of a harmonious union of naturalism and delicate abstraction of form that allows for considerable heightening of detail and, at the same time, a suspended contemplative vision.

ROOM 21

Manifestations of naturalism in Tuscany

In the First Fine Arts Exhibition organised in Leghorn in 1886, apart from the due homage to the fathers of the macchiaioli *(Signorini, Fattori, Lega), much space was devoted to the naturalistic painting of Cecconi, Cannicci, Ferroni and Francesco Gioli, while in the Paris World Fair of 1889, together with the same personages of the early* macchiaioli *school and painters from the generation of the 40s and 50s, younger painters made headway, such as Panerai, Nomellini, Edoardo Gordigiani and Ulvi Liegi, much appreciated by Signorini, who pointed out that their works represented "the conscientious and exact observation of the infinities of forms and characters" translated into roaming volumes and changing luminous effects. The victory attained over the realism of the distant Romantic foundations was also evident in the works of Ruggero Focardi, narrative yet noble and severe, and in those of Filadelfo Simi, veined by symbolist premonitions, not to mention the multiple manifestations of the modern principle of the 'real', which in the century's last years breached the remaining unity of Tuscan figurative culture.*

NICCOLÒ CANNICCI
Thirst in the fields
Oil on canvas, 54 × 45 cm

The topic of the painting, although linked to the campestral subjects typical of Cannicci and very much to the taste of the most learned bourgeois clientele, indicates, in its title, a precise will to adhere to the thematics of verismo. Its composition, on the other hand, represents a monumental form springing from knowledge of both French contemporary painting – which the artist acquired in Paris in 1875 in the company of Fattori, Banti and Ferroni – and the first instances of symbolism which, precisely through a new conception of the 'real', anticipated in art, as well as literature, the time of Decadentism.

ADOLFO TOMMASI
Spring
Oil on canvas, 150 × 200 cm

Acquired at the 1899 Exhibition of the Society of Fine Arts and donated by the king to the Modern Art Gallery, this enormous painting celebrates nature in almost epic forms, according to the sense of formal solemnity that, in the wake of Fattori's teachings, characterises Tuscan painting of the century's end. As occurs in other works by Tommasi, the topic, of evident realistic imprint, here consents expressing – as often happens in so–called 'campestral painting' – symbolist suggestions due to the mysterious solitude of the countryside and the animism, typical of Pascoli, of the vegetable fields.

Room 22

Italian schools of the latter half of the 19th century

In examining the most notable feats in the history of Tuscan art, which up to here has arrived at affirmation of the modern ideas surrounding the concepts of nature and 'truth', it is now necessary to compare all that was going on in the latter half of the century in other regions of Italy, where the same aesthetic debate often found reasons for appraisal or, through the artists, the occasion for fruitful meetings and exchanges. Southern Italy was specially interested, with its Palizzi, Morelli and Mancini, in the direct expression of a truth which was at times radiant, and at others charged with an existential restlessness reflected in works of great suggestiveness for the Tuscans as well. New light, more expressive than natural, colour the paintings of the Roman painters having arisen in the climate of D'Annunzio, depicting a countryside transfigured by barbaric myths; while some would chose the phenomena of nature itself for their turbid majesty, such as for example, the eruptions painted by Netti and De Nittis with spectacular results unknown amongst the measured Tuscan narration.

DOMENICO MORELLI

Meeting in a Constantinople cemetery

Oil on canvas,
46.2 × 71.5 cm

The painting, from 1894, appeared under the title *Memory of youthful rea-* dings at the Festa di Arte e dei Fiori of 1896 – an imposing review of the most significant experiences of international art of the century's end. It is an document of those evocations of the East, coloured by sensuality and nostalgia, that Morelli gave precedence to over the interpretations of a reality otherwise observed through positivist inclemency and inflexible morality of the social 'poets', and which at the century's end was tinged with symbolist inflections.

GIUSEPPE DE NITTIS
Rain of ashes
Oil on wood-plate,
45×30 cm

Carried out in 1872, this painting, typical of Neapolitan iconography, achieved great success, as did other studies of Mount Vesuvius, which De Nittis used as a means for trying out innovations on the countryside and varying atmospheric situations. The painting suggested analogies with the hundreds of views of Mt. Fujiama by Okusai, testament to the artist's vast culture that, in the cosmopolitan atmosphere of Paris, would continue the aesthetic experience of the impressionists, introducing notes of elegant mundanity into the representation of domestic life.

Room 23

Models and influences of Mitteleuropean culture

The last two decades of the century are characterised by the significant influences of European art on Italian culture: from the neo-renaissance aesthetics of the pre-Raphaelite English, to the romantic Hellenism and Mediterranean myths of the German school. These new elements, either assimilated directly by the Italian artists or sparked by foreigners present in Rome and Florence, contributed to inducing a definitive crisis in the principles and forms of Risorgimento realism, displacing aesthetic study toward the obscurest and most disquieting areas of man and the world surrounding him. In the attempt to transfer the artistic cultural problems of the moment ever more towards a mystical and irrational plane, painters and poets discover the mythical origins of contemporary reality, thus populating the Roman countryside and reedbeds of the Arno's mouth with Centaurs, or seeking justification for a risky and alternative existence in the sunny silences of the East.

OTTO VERMEHREN

Paolo and Francesca

Oil on canvas, 152.5 × 97 cm

The work belongs to the mature years of the artist, formed in Weimar and then at the Art Academy of Munich, that is to say, in the ambience of the historicist and symbolist trends of the century's end. This painting is an example of Vermehren's Mitteleuropean style that approached the painting of Feuerbach, the late works of Henner and especially those of Böcklin, who was the artist's close friend in the years 1887 to 1890, during their first stay in Florence: the city where, from 1900 to 1916, he would live with his family, acquiring great prestige as an art restorer and imitator.

EDOARDO GELLI
Portrait of Bruna Pagliano
Oil on canvas,
170.5 × 126 cm

A significant example of the style adopted by Gelli in portraying exponents of the high bourgeoisie, this painting, dated 1904, was rendered spectacular by the frame with its sinuous *Art Nouveau* decorations. The Ligurian artist had been trained at the school of Antonio Ciseri, whence the clear construction of his drawing. However, instead of continuing the austere formalism of his teacher, he soon adapted to the themes favoured by the marketplace, specialising in the genres of moralistic painting and historical-military subjects.

Room 24

Pointillism, Symbolism and social themes

The spiritualistic movements that characterised European culture in the last two decades of the 19th Century – from the symbolism of Gustave Moreau and Odilon Redon to the 'D'Annunzianism' of Sartorio and Michetti – engendered the crisis in the principles of objective reality that is to underlie the naturalistic optimism of the informative painting of the century's final years. These orientations arose as reactions to the inadequacies of Positivism and Verismo and, revealing the feeling of mystery, regarded light and colour as the means to overcome the materiality of things. It was on the basis of these premises, therefore, that the divisionist painting of Nomellini, Previati, Kienerk, the more intensely literary ones of Adolfo Tommasi and Antony De Witt, as well as the same formal disintegration evident in the Medardo Rosso's sculptures, would integrate a contradictory range of values, from mysticism to social intervention, conceived as indivisible categories of the new lyrical spiritualism.

MEDARDO ROSSO
Laughing woman
Bronze, h. 59 cm

The woman's physiognomy, as in other plastic 'snapshots' by the sculptor, arises from a background that defines the perspective and circumscribes the relationships amongst figure, environment and atmosphere, according to compositional canons anticipating the solutions of the new century. The work is dated 1891, according to the author's own indications at the first Italian show on Impressionism in Florence in 1910. It was organised with the intention of countering the dusty luminism of French painters with the formal synthesis of Cézanne's painting, by which even the vigorous definition of sculptural planes of Rosso seemed to abide.

GAETANO PREVIATI
In the meadow
Oil on canvas, 61 × 55 cm

Carried out between 1880 and 1890, the painting was exhibited at the 10th Biennial of Venice (1912) and acquired by the Minister Credaro for the Florence Modern Art Gallery, which thereby came into possession of one of the Emilian painter's most significant works. The painting, also known as *Morning and Children in the meadow*, signals the decisive stage in Previati's conversion to the technique of pointillism and demonstrates the artist's vocation for wide and luminous spaces and a variety of chromatic combinations that correspond perfectly to the high concept of 'decoration' as conceived by symbolist poetics.

PLINIO NOMELLINI
Little Bacchus
Oil on canvas, 121 × 94 cm

This painting was presented at the 1910 Venice Biennial and probably depicts Nomellini's own son, transfigured by the artist's fantasies of Pan. On that occasion, Vittorio Pica underscored the painter's capacity to unify "purposeful audacity in technique with noble grace in composition", recognising the work as the culmination of the symbolist vein already brilliantly enunciated in *Ditirambo*, also exhibited in Venice in 1905. Although contained within his experimentation on the *tocco diviso* (divided brush strokes), the aestheticism with which Nomellini evokes the appearance of the young god remains evident and recalls the classicism of Sartorio and De Carolis.

ROOMS 25, 26

Study collections

These two rooms are given over to holding temporary exhibitions of the works conserved in the museum's inventory, new acquisitions, especially significant collections and small showings of subjects akin to the themes of 19th and 20th-century art in the Gallery's holdings.

THE COLLECTION OF EMILIO GAGLIARDINI

Composed of for forty-three paintings, most of which are by the most famous exponents of macchiaioli *painting (Fattori, Lega, Signorini, Borrani, Abbati, Banti, Cabianca, D'Ancona, Di Tivoli, Costa and Sernesi), this collection, for it aesthetic value and historical significance, represents one of the most excellent and well-known examples of Italian collecting of our century. The critical rigor and the taste with which the collector performed his selections make viewing this collection a required and irreplaceable step for studying and understanding the important Tuscan realist movement. Created by the industrialist Emilio Gagliardini in the second post-war period, the collection offers the opportunity to admire a series of masterpieces that had remained unseen for some time. Some of them hold particular significance within the overall production of their respective authors. Paintings, like* Horses in Tombolo *by Fattori,* The spring roses *by Lega and* Children in the sun *by Signorini, represent focal points within the whole collection and evince a goal in the creative parable of these artists. Their current arrangement in the Modern Art Gallery of Pitti Palace, possible by virtue of the commodate consenting their exhibition to the*

public, further enrich the Florentine collections with extraordinary testimonies to the schools of Castiglioncello and Piagentina. Together with works of such renowned Maestri, the collection has included a number of artists from the generation immediately following the macchiaioli. *From the 'Leghorn School' come a number of paintings already well-known to the public, such as Oscar Ghiglia's* The Mirror *and Nomellini's* Noon.

GIOVANNI FATTORI
Horses in the pine wood of Tombolo
Oil on canvas, 85 × 174 cm

The painting is from the artist's most prolific years, between 1866 and 1867. While living in the vicinity of Leghorn, Fattori experimented with a style based on the study of space and rigorous construction of natural elements. It was this that allowed him to overcome the compositional aspects without however neglecting the effects of lighting and its incidence on the landscape, in accordance with the rural spiritualism of Millet and the Barbizon painters.

TELEMACO SIGNORINI

Expulsion of the Austrians from the village of Solferino

Oil on canvas,
61.5 × 120 cm

This is the largest of the five works painted by Signorini between 1859 and 1861 in a theme from the Risorgimento. It was exhibited at the Promotrice of Florence in 1861 and later at the first National Exhibition, where it received a medal and was acquired by Isabella Falconer. The reality of the scene, accented by the extraordinary effect of the storm, follows from the studies that Signorini carried out directly on the grounds of war, even being arrested under suspicion of espionage.

ODOARDO BORRANI

The mournful news

Oil on canvas, 110 × 138 cm

The subject of the painting still belongs to the climate of the Risorgimento and represents a young girl, seated at a table lighted by an oil lamp, reading the newspaper to two women emotionally moved by the news of the death of

Vittorio Emanuele II. Borrani worked on the painting in 1880, and in it appeals to a solemn and intense composition that demonstrates his having transcended the formal *macchiaioli* tradition in favour of themes and atmospheres drawn most likely from French contemporary painting.

Plinio Nomellini
Noon

Oil on canvas, 198 × 198 cm

In this work of monumental dimensions, Nomellini develops one of the subjects that best fit his sensibilities, refined as they were by literary interests and a cult of the emotions that would frequently lead him to depict his family in scenes of subtle emotional involvement. The artist had just risen from the table in order to capture the beautiful tree-filtered light of a summer's midday; thus confirming the talent of this, 'the solar painter' in exploiting the technique of the *tocco diviso* to render powerful luminous irradiation.

ROOM 27

Figurative Tuscan culture surrounding "Il Marzocco" and "Leonardo"

The 20th Century commences in Florence with a vitality that assimilates the drive for emancipation from the aesthetics of the late 19th Century and the strong aspirations of its artists to appropriate the newly arisen European tendencies in antagonism to the cultural sediment of the century just ended. In the magazine "Il Marzocco", this appeal to progress was concretised in the cosmopolitan vision of Ugo Ojetti and aesthetic eclecticism represented by the 'D'Annunzian' milieu, which would attract young artists like Soffici and Costetti, and others like Armando Spadini, bound to each other by an intellectual aristocracy, declared in the elegant pages of "Leonardo" and the refined circle of their supporters, headed by Giovanni Papini.

ARMANDO SPADINI

Confidences

Oil on canvas, 107 × 100 cm

This work, which can be dated to between 1919 and 1922, documents the period in which the artist, leaving behind the works that he himself defined as "sketches and impressions", begins to manifest a clear tendency toward demanding composition, thus reacting to the criticism levelled at him by the theorists of the return to order, who demanded monumentality and formal rigour in art. This poetic change earned Spadini admission to the group of Plastic Values in the Florentine Primaverile of 1922, where his painting was praised for its healthy character and freedom from 'cerebralism'.

OSCAR GHIGLIA

Portrait of Giovanni Papini

Oil on canvas, 66 × 57 cm

This incomplete portrait was executed in the second decade of the 20th century, when Papini became interested in the painting of the Leghorn artist, writing an article in "Vita d'arte" in 1908 that regarded precisely Ghiglia's work as a portrait-artist and his sound knowledge of post-impressionism French art. After sharing the enthusiasm of the artistic and literary adventures linked to "Leonardo" and "La Voce", the two would pass on to a dignified, though hostile estrangement that would for a long time place them on diametrically opposed sides of the debate regarding avant-garde futurism and the autonomy of art.

ROOM 28

European influences on Tuscan art of the second decade of the 20th century

On the occasion of the show of the "Leghorn impressionists" of 1891, Giovanni Fattori expressed concern and disappointment upon seeing that his young pupils had distanced themselves from the solid structures created by the mac-chiaioli tradition and given themselves over to rash combinations of tones, following the example of the contemporary post-impressionist currents. The exhibition, that brought together Nomellini, Muller and Kienerk, amongst others, actually signalled that the provincial post-macchiaioli approach had been surpassed, thanks to the timely awareness by these painters of the Secessionist movement and the figurative results born of critical reflections on impressionist art. On the other hand, Fattori could not know to what extent his own work, carried to its extreme, as essential and analogical as the painting of Cézanne, would influence some artists of the early 20th century, mainly Oscar Ghiglia and other Tuscans who, by the same means and thanks to the critical zeal of Soffici and Ojetti, learned to understand the spirit of the European avant-garde.

LORENZO VIANI

Self-portrait

Oil on canvas, 98 × 67 cm

This self-portrait, dated between 1910 and 1912, corresponds to the description of the restless artist offered by Ettore Cozzani, director of the magazine "L'Eroica", on which Viani collaborated as xylographer in 1914: "a strange scruffy and impetuous sort of savage ... a provocative and sarcastic rebel". Concerning the style, the painter addresses Mitteleuropean culture, interpreting in an original and unembellished fashion the *fauve* and expressionist languages, with references to Nolde, Die Brücke, Munch and Barlach, whom Viani had purposely chosen so as to underscore the noncon-formist and anarchical positions that he would hold throughout his life.

GIUSEPPE VINER
The mine
Oil on canvas, 128 × 143 cm

The painter, strongly tied to the land of his origins, very often worked on subjects that illustrated the scenes and events related to the quarries of Carrara, achieving spectacular results through their resolution in an abstracting and chromatically vibrant style, very akin to some of the figurative aspects of the Viennese Secession. The controlled balance between nature and decoration present in this painting is moreover the result of Viner's training, beginning at the Industrial Arts School of Florence and continuing through his work as decorator in Tuscany, where the ornamental fashion of Galileo Chini was held in the utmost regard.

GALILEO CHINI

Peace

Oil on canvas,
199 × 126.5 cm

This was carried out, along with the two other paintings, *Indolence* and *Faith*, between 1911 and 1914, during Chini's travels in Siam, where he had gone to fresco the throne room of the Royal Palace in Bangkok. On his return from East China he would accentuate the evocative aspects of his divisionist formation, participating in the Venice Biennial of 1914 with a series of paintings wholly comparable to the most significant examples of European Symbolism, and from then on cultivating a style of great literary suggestion, which called for the collaboration of modernist poets and musicians believing in the syncretism of the arts.

Legacy of Mai Sewell Costetti

This room is dedicated to the paintings of Giovanni Costetti bequeathed to the Gallery by the painter's widow, a Norwegian citizen, journalist and ceramist. Her last will and testament stipulated that the works left in her possession were to be donated to the museums of the cities most linked to her husband's activities: Florence, Reggio Emilia, Settignano and Bergen. Of the thirty works received, this selection represents the most important, and most suitable to delineating Costetti's personality: idealist, tending towards mysticism, but also attentive to the evolution of the 20th-century aesthetic aimed at recovering the values of Cézanne and the return of order.

GIOVANNI COSTETTI
*The good smile
(The French woman)*
Oil on canvas, 120 × 95 cm

Dated to around 1903, the painting depicts perhaps the painter Beatrice Ancillotti and was exhibited for the first time at the Biennial of Venice in 1912, entered with the title of *The good smile*. The work represents a high level of the artist's adhesion, in his youth, to the symbolist culture and international secessionism of the early part of the century, a culture which he could have become directly acquainted with during his stay in Paris in 1900. In those same years, Costetti collaborates on the magazine "Leonardo" and keeps the company of artists and writers – D'Annunzio, De Carolis, Andreotti and Kienerk – that further stimulate his interest in the European horizon, as also evident in this portrait, very akin to certain pastels by Fernand Knopff.

Giovanni Costetti
Girl on the balcony
(At the terrace)
Oil on cardboard,
50 × 33 cm

The painting probably originates from the years in which the artist became especially interested in the works of German Expressionism which he had opportunity to view at the Third Show of the Secession in Rome in 1915 and the Venice Biennial of 1922, where the figurative current was amply represented. Indeed, a drawing by Munch exhibited in Rome, entitled *The two*, even seems to have constituted a certain precedent for this painting, which moreover indicates its having been executed between 1915 and 1920.

GIOVANNI COSTETTI
Self-portrait with pupil Domenico Candia

Oil on cardboard,
70 × 58 cm

This is one of the numerous portraits that Costetti performed using as a model his pupil, Domenico Candia, who himself exhibited for the first time, together with his teacher, in the Florentine Primaverile of 1922. Possibly done in that same year, the work demonstrates the attention that Costetti devoted to the renaissance tradition and his awareness of fixing within a portrait, through erudite references, an almost heroic moment, which was in any event, relevant to his own experience and the culture of the moment and saw him as the interpreter of the European avant-garde.

Room 30

Acquisitions at the Florentine Primaverile of 1922

In 1922 Florence hosted important exhibitions dedicated to the art of the 17th and 18th Centuries, a fact that underscored the renewed interest in studying those centuries which had until then been despised. It was also the site of an important, wide-ranging contemporary art review aimed at recapitulating the national artistic research of the post-war era and, almost in syntony with the rediscovery of Caravaggio and Mattia Preti, finding the way to rejoin tradition indicating, amongst others, the 19th century Italians - commemorated through the homage of Lega and Signorini - as an ulterior area for aesthetic inquiry. The choice of artists invited to the Tuscan Primaverile substantially reflected this planned return to the form and noble models of Italian art. Thus, amongst the choices were the much appreciated 'purified naturalism' of Baccio Maria Bacci, the architectural sense of Libero Andreotti, the impressive realism of Evaristo Boncinelli, the inlays of pure colour by Arturo Checchi and the devotion of Fattori's pupils to Cézanne, which the review gathered together for the first time, trenchantly recording the contributions of the new generation within the Tuscan setting.

EVARISTO BONCINELLI
Head of old man (Contadino)
Marble, h. 32 cm

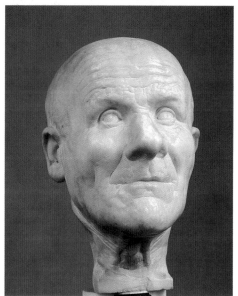

This version in marble was cast from the plaster mould, also in the collection of the Modern Art Gallery, displayed at the First Tuscan Winter Exhibition of 1914-1915. The sculptor, who suffered from psychic imbalance and tended to represent human misery, sculpted the face of the old man with a sharp realism that finds its roots in the more Hellenic examples of Roman sculpture and the rough and vivid figures of Etruscan art. These would be the models recovered in the 20th Century through the expressive force that its artists would couple with a return to the strong original substance of Italian art.

RENATO NATALI
*Quarter (via
Buontalenti)*
Oil on canvas, 190 × 150 cm

The painting stands out
in monumental form
amongst the many
'masquerades balls'
and 'brawls' that Natali
imagined by uniting ob-
servation of reality with
the signs and colours
matured during his ex-
periences with the Tus-
can post-*macchiaioli*
and avant-garde Paris,
where the painter
moved in 1914, also ad-
hering to the graphic
tastes of Leonetto Cap-
piello. The scenograph-
ic cut of the painting is
indeed sustained by a
graphic layout of great
solidity, while the
colour defines the form,
exalting its expressive
value with effective
emergence of tones that
recall the pictorial ex-
pressiveness of the
peintres de rues of the
19th and 20th centuries.

INDEX OF ARTISTS AND WORKS

Luigi Catani, Decoration, room 11.

printed in May 1999
by Media Print-Livorno
for
s i l l a b e